Siamese Cats as Pets

A Complete Owner's Guide to Siamese Cats and Kittens

Including Types of Siamese Cats, Facts, Names, Breeds, Colors, Personality, Information about Owning and Choosing a Siamese Cat Breeder and Rescue

Wendy Davis

Published by Atticus Publications

© 2014 Atticus Publications

Printed and bound in Great Britain by Lightning Source.

Foreword

This book is designed to provide you with answers to your most pressing questions about Siamese Cats. Here you will learn everything from the history of the breed to facts about what to feed Siamese Cats and how to care for them. Because this book is written in a clear and easy-to-read fashion, you will find it a joy to read. By the time you finish this book you will have a good idea whether or not the Siamese Cat is a good choice for you and your family – you will also have a firm foundation of knowledge to prepare you for owning and caring for your cat.

Table of Contents

Chapter One: Introduction

The Siamese Cat is one of the most easily identifiable breeds of cat, but how much do you really know about them? These cats appear in popular culture in movies such as Disney's *Lady and the Tramp* and in books like Sheila Burnford's novel *The Incredible Journey*. If you were to see a Siamese Cat in the pet store, you would almost certainly be able to identify it.

If you are considering keeping a Siamese Cat as a pet, however, you will need to know more than just what this breed looks like. You will need to learn the basics about their nutritional requirements, how to care for them and what to do if they get sick. Owning a cat is a big responsibility and not something that you should enter into lightly. That is where this book comes in.

In this book you will find answers to your most pressing questions about Siamese Cats. What do Siamese Cats eat? Do these cats get along well with dogs and other pets? Is a Siamese Cat a good choice for a family with children? You will find the answers to all of these questions and more within the pages of this book. By the time you finish this book you will have a good idea whether or not the Siamese Cat is a good choice for you and your family – you will also have a firm foundation of knowledge to prepare you for owning and caring for your cat.

Useful Terms to Know

Albino (albinism) – a mutation in animals resulting in little to no pigmentation (color) in the eyes, skin and coat

Blue – a color used to describe a cat's coat; not true blue but a slate gray color

Breed Standard – the desired characteristics of a breed set forth by cat associations such as the CFA

CFA – the Cat Fanciers' Association, Inc.; the primary cat association in the United States

Cobby – a compact body shape

Color Points – a color pattern in which certain points of the body (face, ears, legs and tail) have a darker coloration than the rest of the body

Congenital – inherited; a condition present at birth

Dam – the female parent of a litter; mother

Declawing – the surgical removal of a cat's claw and first joint, including the bones and ligaments

Gestation – pregnancy; the period during which the kittens develop in the womb of the female cat before birth

Hybrid – a crossing of two different breeds

Inbreeding – the breeding of related cats within a closed group; ex: breeding mother to son, sister to brother

Kink – a misshapen vertebra in the tail

Kitten – a baby cat; a cat under 9 months of age

Litter – a family of kittens born to one mother at the same time

Milk Kneading – a treading motion a kitten makes to stimulate milk flow when nursing

Outcross – breeding of one cat to an unrelated cat

Sire – the male parent of a cat; father

Spay – the surgical process of sterilizing a female cat, rendering her incapable of pregnancy

TICA – the International Cat Association, a worldwide genetic registry for cat owners

Tom – an intact male cat

Tortoiseshell – a coat pattern that consists of a mosaic of red, cream and another base color (blue, cinnamon, chocolate, etc.)

Wean – introducing kittens to solid food as a replacement for milk

Chapter Two: Understanding Siamese Cats

The Siamese Cat is a very old breed of domestic cat and one that continues to be fairly popular all over the world. This breed is known as much for its unique appearance as for its playful nature which makes it a great family pet. If you are considering a Siamese Cat for yourself or your family, take the time to learn the basics about the breed first. In this chapter you will learn what makes these cats unique as well as their history and other fun facts.

1.) What Are Siamese Cats?

The Siamese Cat is a breed of domestic cat known for its long, lithe body and color points. One of several cat breeds native to Thailand, the Siamese Cat was one of the first Oriental breeds to be recognized. The Thai name for this cat is Wichianmat, which translates to "moon diamond," perhaps in reference to the vivid blue color of the cat's eyes or the shape of the color pointed mask on its face.

According to The International Cat Association (TICA), the Siamese Cat is a social and intelligent breed that loves to play and interact with its family well into adulthood. In fact, many Siamese owners claim that their pets exhibit many dog-like qualities in their love of play and cravings for attention. Some Siamese Cats have even been known to play games of fetch with their owners.

Fun Fact: Siamese Cats are often nicknamed "Meezer" due to their vocal tendencies. These cats have a loud, low-pitched voice but they are capable of producing cries that sound like a human baby when they want attention.

2.) Facts about Siamese Cats

Siamese Cats are medium-sized, typically achieving an adult weight between 8 and 12 pounds (3.6 to 5.4 kg), though females tend to stay at the lower end of the spectrum. These cats have a long, lithe body that is almost tubular in shape, though the muscles are clearly defined. Siamese Cats have wedge-shaped heads that form a triangle between the tip of the nose and the ears.

These cats have very short, sleek coats of fine hair that has a glossy texture. Though Siamese Cats do not tend to shed much, regular brushing is recommended to keep the coat in good health. The most common coat color for this breed is white or cream, often shading to a lighter tone around the stomach. The defining characteristic of Siamese Cats, however, is their color points – areas of darker color on the face (mask), legs, ears and tail. These points may come in a variety of colors including seal, chocolate, blue, lilac, red, tabby or tortoise-shell.

The pointed pattern exhibited by Siamese Cats is actually a form of albinism which results from a mutated tyrosinase enzyme. All Siamese kittens are born cream-colored or white but they develop darker color points over the first few months of life. These points develop at the colder points of the body – the areas that receive less blood flow. This is because the mutated tyrosinase enzyme is heat-sensitive – it fails to work at normal body temperature but activates in cooler areas. In addition to developing color points, Siamese Cats also tend to darken in color with age. Interestingly, cats living in warmer climates tend to retain lighter coats than those living in colder climates.

Summary of Facts

Scientific Classification: *Felis catus* (domestic cat)

Size: medium-sized

Weight: 8 to 12 lbs. (3.6 to 5.4 kg)

Body Shape: long and lithe, graceful, triangular-shaped head and a thin, tapered tail

Coat Length: short, lies close to body

Coat Texture: fine, glossy

Shedding: low

Grooming: very easy, only requires brushing

Colors: four colors accepted by CFA – seal point, chocolate point, blue point, lilac point

Eye Color: deep vivid blue

Temperament: extremely affectionate and social, love being around people

Lifespan: average 10 to 13 years

Interaction with Children: gets along well with children, likes to play

Interaction with Pets: generally gets along well with cat-friendly dogs

General Health: higher rate of mortality compared to other breeds, several common diseases

Intelligence: very intelligent

Playfulness: very playful and active

3.) History of Siamese Cats as Pets

The exact origins of the Siamese Cat are unknown, but it is generally thought to be one of several breeds that originated in Siam (now Thailand). Mentions of pale, color-pointed cats can be traced back to the 1300s in ancient Siamese manuscripts called Tamra Maew, or Cat Poems. These cats were said to have pale-colored bodies with darker color points on the face, tail, feet and ears.

The Siamese Cat made its debut in England in 1871 at the first cat show held at the Crystal Palace in London. At the time, the breed was not well received – attendees of the show thought that the Siamese was unnatural, a "nightmare kind of cat". The popularity of the breed began to increase, however, when the first specimen of the breed was brought to the United States in 1878. President Rutherford B. Hayes received the first Siamese Cat to enter the U.S. as a gift from the American Consul in Bangkok – he named the cat Siam.

Several years after the first Siamese Cat arrived in the U.S., the British Consul-General in Bangkok brought a breeding pair back to Britain as a gift to his sister, Lilian Jane Gould. Gould went on to co-found the Siamese Cat Club several years later in 1901. By 1885, Gould's pair had produced three kittens which were then shown at the Crystal Palace show that same year. Unfortunately, the kittens died shortly after the show.

In 1886, a second pair of Siamese Cats was imported into the U.K. This pair of cats differed from the first pair in several key ways – they were slightly larger but had a less "cobby" body type. These cats had wedge-shaped muzzles and larger, more pointed ears. These physical differences set the Siamese Cat apart from traditional Western breeds and left a lasting impression. Over the years that followed, more specimens of the breed were imported to form the base breeding pool for Siamese Cats in Britain. In fact, it is thought that all of the Siamese Cats in Britain today are descendant from the original breeding pool which consisted of eleven cats.

During the early years of breed development, Siamese Cats were called the "Royal Cat of Siam." Over the years, the breed continued to increase in popularity and by the 1950s there was a movement toward favoring a sleek and slender look in the breed. Selective breeding practices resulted in a long, fine-boned cat with a narrow wedge-shaped head and large almond-shaped eyes. By the 1980s, the original form of the breed had all but disappeared from cat shows in favor of the slimmer modern type.

Today there are two "types" of Siamese Cat – the traditional Siamese and the modern "show" style. TICA and the World Cat Federation also accept a breed known as the Thai, a less extreme variation of the Siamese Cat. These cats are also known by the names Old Style Siamese, Classic Siamese and Applehead. Though the body shape and style of the Siamese Cat has largely been standardized between the U.S. and the U.K., there are still differences in regard to accepted colors. The Cat Fanciers' Association (CFA) in the U.S. only accepts four colors (seal, chocolate, blue and lilac point) while TICA accepts red, tabby and tortoise-shell color points in addition to these four colors.

4.) Colors of Siamese Cats

According to the Cat Fanciers' Association. (CFA), there are four acceptable colors for Siamese Cats. These colors include the following:

- Seal point
- Chocolate point
- Blue point
- Lilac point

Though these four colors are the only variations accepted by the CFA, other colors are possible. Outcrossing Siamese Cats with other breeds may result in a red or cream point, a lynx (tabby) point or even a tortoise-shell point. In the UK, Siamese Cats exhibiting these colorations are considered part of the same breed but the CFA in the United States does not. Cats having colors other than the four listed above are considered Oriental cats or Colorpoint Shorthairs by the CFA in the United States.

a.) Seal Point

Seal point Siamese Cats exhibit a body color that is pale cream or fawn, gradually shading to a lighter tone on the chest and stomach. The points are deep seal brown in color. Nose leather and paw pads should be the same color as the points and the eyes should be a deep vivid blue.

b.) Chocolate Point

Chocolate point Siamese Cats have an ivory color on the body with no shading. The points are a warm milk-chocolate in color. The nose and paw pads should be cinnamon-pink and the eyes a deep vivid blue.

c.) Blue Point

Blue point Siamese cats have a body color that is blueish white with a cold tone. The shading is gradual, fading to white on the stomach and chest. The points are deep blue in color with slate-colored nose leather and paw pads. The eyes are deep vivid blue.

d.) Lilac Point

Lilac point Siamese Cats have glacial white coloring on the body with no shading. The points are a frosty grey color with a pinkish tone. The nose leather and paw pads are lavender-pink in color, the eyes deep vivid blue.

Chapter Three: What to Know Before You Buy

Now that you know the basics about Siamese Cats, you may have a good idea whether or not this is the right breed for you. Before you go out and buy a cat, however, you should take the time to consider some of the more practical aspects of cat ownership. Will you need to license your cat? Will he get along with your other pets? How much does it cost to keep a cat? You will find the answers to these questions and more in this chapter.

1.) Do You Need a License?

If you have ever owned a dog, you are probably familiar with the licensing process for pets. But you may be wondering whether the same rules apply to cats. Unfortunately, licensing requirements for cats can be a little confusing as there is no overarching federal requirement for licensing cats in the United States or in the U.K. Before you go out and buy a Siamese Cat, however, you would be wise to apprise yourself of local and regional requirements regarding the licensing of cats.

a.) Licensing in the U.S.

As it has already been mentioned, there are no federal requirements in the United States for cat owners to license their pets. For the most part, this type of legislature is set forth at the state or local level. While there are strict requirements for licensing exotic pets and big cats, the rules for licensing cats are much more relaxed. In fact, the only U.S. state that requires cat owners to license their cats is Rhode Island.

Even if your state does not require you to license your cat, however, you should still consider doing so. In licensing your cat you will be providing the state with proof of ownership as well as your contact information – this will come in handy if your cat ever gets lost. Of course, this information will only be useful if you put a collar and ID tag on your cat. This is particularly important for outdoor cats, though indoor cats may be fine without a license.

b.) Licensing in the U.K.

Similar to the U.S., there are no overarching requirements in the U.K. stating that cat owners must license their pets. There are, however, strict rules regarding the import and export of cats (including U.K. residents who are traveling with their cats). You should also be aware that in 2006 the Animal Welfare Act was passed which requires pet owners to provide suitable accommodations, food and companionship for their pets. This act does not require licensing – just proper care of pets.

2.) How Many Should You Buy?

While many cats are capable of getting along with others, Siamese Cats actually prefer to be kept in pairs or groups. These cats are very social by nature and may get lonely or depressed if they do not receive enough attention. If you work during the day or spend a lot of time away from home, it is important that you provide your Siamese Cat with a playmate to keep him company.

3.) Can Siamese Cats Be Kept with Other Pets?

Siamese Cats are generally very friendly which means that they get along with just about everyone – including other pets. Not only are these cats good with children, but they are also likely to get along with cat-friendly dogs. The only time a Siamese Cat will not get along with a dog is if that dog has a strong prey drive and tends to chase the cat around the house. If your dog is used to cats, however, or he has a calm temperament then there should be no problems.

If you have small animals in the house such as hamsters or guinea pigs, it would be wise for you to keep the cage out of your cat's reach. A Siamese Cat is likely to view small rodents like hamsters and mice as prey or playthings, though guinea pigs may be less of an issue. If you have a fish tank, it is important that you keep it tightly covered so your cat is not tempted to go fishing.

4.) Ease and Cost of Care

When it comes to keeping Siamese Cats, they are generally not difficult to keep. Like any pet, these cats require a nutritious diet, a safe place to live and plenty of affection and attention from their owners. In addition to considering the ease of keeping this type of cat, however, you also need to think about the associated costs. In this section you will learn what kind of costs you can expect initially and on a monthly basis for Siamese Cats – you will also receive an explanation and estimate for each cost.

a.) Initial Costs

The initial costs for a Siamese Cat include those costs which you must cover before you bring the cat home. These costs include the purchase price of the cat as well as the costs for spay and surgery, microchipping, vaccinations, a cat carrier, food/water bowls, a litter box and cat toys.

Purchase Price = The purchase price for Siamese Cats will vary greatly depending where you get them. If you purchase purebred CFA or TICA registered kittens from a reputable breeder, you can expect to pay between $500 and $700 (£325 - £455) for each kitten. If you purchase your kitten from a pet store or a hobby breeder, the cost may be less – between $200 and $400 (£130 - £260). If you are not concerned with pedigree, you may also be able to find Siamese Cats at your local cat rescue or shelter with an adoption fee under $100 (£65).

Spay/Neuter = Unless you plan to breed your Siamese Cat, it is wise to have it spayed or neutered. Having your cat spayed or neutered will help to prevent unwanted litters and, in female cats, it will help you to avoid the mess of your cat going into heat. The average cost for spay surgery is between $100 and $200 (£75 to £150) while neutering may cost as little as $50 to $100 (£37 to £75).

Microchipping = There is no federal or state requirement for cat owners to have their pets microchipped, but it is definitely something you should consider. Having your cat microchipped ensures that if he gets lost, whoever finds him will be able to contact you (as long as your information is up to date). The average cost for having your cat microchipped by a licensed vet is around $50 (£32.50).

Vaccinations = If you purchase a kitten from a reputable breeder, it should already be up to date on its vaccinations. If you purchase an older cat, however, you may need to take it to the vet for booster shots. The cost for vaccinations will vary depending how many your cat needs, but you should budget for a cost between $50 and $100 (£37 to £75).

Cat Carrier = A crate or cat carrier is what you will use to transport your cat when you take him outside the house. The average cost for a cat carrier is around $40 (£30).

Food/Water Bowls = Cats are generally not picky when it comes to their food and water bowls, but you have the option to choose something decorative if you like. A set of simple stainless steel food and water bowls should cost you no more than $15 (£11).

Litter Box = When it comes to buying a litter box for your cat, you have many options. A basic litter box may only cost you $10 (£7.5) while a fancier model could be in the range of $40 (£30) or more. Plan to spend about $20 (£15) on a litter box for your cat so you can get one with a lid to help control the odor.

Grooming Supplies = Siamese Cats have very short coats that require little more than regular brushing. This being the case, you do not need to invest in any expensive grooming supplies – a simple bristle brush will do. The cost for this should be no more than $10 (£6.50).

Cat Toys = Do not feel like you have to spend a lot of money on cat toys because there are many toys that you can make yourself. It is also likely that your cat will play with things like bottle caps and toilet paper tubes, thus negating the need to buy fancy toys. If you want to buy toys for your cat, however, you can expect to spend about $15 (£9.75) for a good assortment to get you started.

Cost Type	One Cat	Two Cats
Purchase Price	$200 - $700 (£130 - £455)	$400 - $1,400 (£260 - £910)
Spay/Neuter	$50 - $200 (£37 - £150)	$100 - $400 (£75 - £300)
Microchipping	$50 (£32.50)	$100 (£65)
Vaccinations	$50 - $100 (£37 - £75)	$100 - $200 (£75 - £150)
Cat Carrier	$40 (£30)	$40 (£30)

Food/Water Bowls	$15 (£11)	$15 (£11)
Litter Box	$20 (£15)	$40 (£30)
Grooming Supplies	$10 (£6.50)	$10 (£6.50)
Cat Toys	$15 (£9.75)	$15 (£9.75)
Total:	$450 - $1,150 (£650 - £1,250)	$820 - $2,220 (£533 - £1,443)

b.) Monthly Costs

The monthly costs for keeping a Siamese Cat include those costs which you must cover on a monthly basis. These costs may include food, flea medication, veterinary care, cat litter and other costs. You will find an explanation and estimate for each cost below.

Food = The cost of food is the most significant cost you will have to cover on a monthly basis. Though Siamese Cats are fairly small, they do require two meals a day. Do not be tempted to save money by purchasing cheap food – this may contribute to health problems which will only cost you more in the long run. For one cat, you can expect to pay about $20 (£13) per month on food.

Flea/Tick Medications = Especially if your cat spends any time outside, it would be wise to protect him with a topical flea/tick medications. These medications typically cost around $10 (£6.50) per month.

Veterinary Check-Ups = You will not need to take your cat to the vet every month, but one or two annual visits is recommended. For the sake of budgeting, however, you can divide the cost of these visits over twelve months. A single visit shouldn't cost you much more than $50 (£32.50) which averages to about $4 (£2.60) per month.

Cat Litter = Your monthly costs for cat litter depends on the type of litter you buy and how many cats you have. If you have only one cat and purchase basic clumping cat litter, you can expect to spend around $20 (£13) per month.

Other Costs = In addition to the monthly costs already mentioned, you may want to factor in some extra money for unexpected costs. These are costs that may not occur every month, but you should be prepared for them just in case. Some costs included in this category may be replacement toys, new collars as your kitten grows, and other minor expenses. Just to be safe, you should budget around $10 (£6.50) per month for these costs.

Cost Type	One Cat	Two Cats
Food	$20 (£13)	$40 (£26)
Flea/Tick Medications	$10 (£6.50)	$20 (£13)
Cat Litter	$20 (£13)	$40 (£26)
Veterinary Check-Ups	$4 (£2.60)	$8 (£5.20)
Other Costs	$10 (£6.5)	$10 (£6.5)
Total:	$65 - $80 (£49 - £60)	$118 - $158 (£88 - £118)

5.) Pros and Cons of Siamese Cats

Before you make your final decision regarding whether or not to buy a Siamese Cat, you would be wise to consider the pros and cons. Each breed of cat has its own unique characteristics and temperament, so they may not all be a good choice for your particular family. Below you will find a list of the pros and cons for the Siamese Cat to help you make an educated decision.

Pros for Siamese Cats

- Very affectionate with family, good with children
- Tend to get along well with cat-friendly dogs and other household pets
- Highly intelligent breed, can learn to play games
- Very unique appearance, comes in a variety of colors
- Short coat sheds little and is easy to groom
- Fairly small breed, only weighs up to 12 lbs. (5.4 kg)

Cons for Siamese Cats

- Require a great deal of attention – may not be a good choice if you spend a lot of time away from home

- Can be very vocal and noisy at times, especially when they want attention
- Lower lifespan than many cat breeds, higher rate of mortality and morbidity
- Generally recommended that they be kept in pairs or groups, not as a single cat

Chapter Four: Purchasing Siamese Cats

Now that you have decided that a Siamese Cat is the right choice for your family, you may be ready to think about actually buying one. Deciding where you buy a cat is a very important decision that could impact the rest of your cat's life. If you do not purchase from a reputable breeder, you may end up with a cat that is not genetically sound and likely to develop health problems later down the line. Do yourself a favor and do some research to find a reputable breeder when it comes time to buy.

1.) Where to Buy Siamese Cats

You may be able to find Siamese Cats and kittens at your local pet store once in a while, but you should ask yourself whether this is truly the best option. In buying from a pet store you cannot be sure where the kittens came from and what their genetic history is like. Siamese Cats in particular are prone to a number of congenital conditions, so you want to be sure that they were responsibly bred to reduce the chances of your cat developing one of these conditions. In this section you will find recommendations for finding a reputable Siamese Cat breeder.

a.) Buying in the U.S.

Even though it is generally not recommended that you purchase kittens from a pet store, you can still use pet stores as a resource. Here you may be able to find recommendations for local breeders or get connected to local rescues. Another place you might look for breeder recommendations is local veterinarians. If all else fails, performing a simple online search for Siamese Cat breeders in your area is likely to return good results.

Here are some Siamese Cat breeders to get you started in your search:

TICA – Siamese Cat Breeders.

<http://www.tica.org/public/breeds/si/breeders.php>

CFA – Cat Breeder Search.

<http://secure.cfa.org/Search.aspx>

Fanciers Breed Referral List.

<http://www.breedlist.com/breeders/sia_ac.html>

Siamese Cat Breeders – CatChannel.com.

<http://www.catchannel.com/classifieds/clsads.aspx?breedname=siamese>

Life with Siamese Cat Breeders Directory.

<http://www.life-with-siamese-cats.com/siamese-cat-breeders.html>

b.) Buying in the U.K.

To find Siamese Cat breeders in the U.K., try some of the links provided below:

The Siamese Cat Society of Scotland.

<http://www.siamese-scotland.co.uk/kitten-and-breeder-list/browse-categories/>

The Siamese Cat Club.

<http://www.siamesecatclub.co.uk/index.htm>

The Midshires Siamese Cat Associations Breeders List.

<http://www.midshiressiamesecatassociation.co.uk/breeders.php>

The Traditional Siamese Cat Association Breeders List.

<http://tsca.uk.tripod.com/Breeders/breeders.htm>

2.) Selecting a Reputable Breeder

Do not be tempted to buy from the first breeder you come across – it is important that you take the time to ascertain the breeder's knowledge and experience. If you purchase from an inexperienced breeder, it is likely that the breeding stock was not of good quality which will increase the chances that the kittens are unhealthy or not genetically sound. Using the resources provided in the previous pages, collect a list of several breeders in your area then go down the list, narrowing it down to select a single breeder.

To narrow down your list of breeders in order to find the best fit, follow these steps:

1. Compile a list of breeders in your area and accumulate as much information as you can about them – this includes contact information, websites and referrals

2. Check the breeder's website – look for reviews from previous customers as well as pictures and information about their breeding stock

3. Look to see if the breeder is registered with TICA or the CFA (depending where you live) – if they are, this information is likely to be posted on the website

4. Call each of the breeders and speak to them personally to ascertain their knowledge and experience

5. Ask the breeder questions about his experience with the Siamese Cat breed as well as his breeding experience in general

6. Keep in mind that a good breeder (one who is concerned about finding a good home for his cats) will likely ask you questions as well

7. Remove from your list any breeders that refuse to answer questions as well as those that do not appear to

be knowledgeable about the breed

8. Make appointments to visit the breeding facilities left on your list – at this point you should have narrowed it down to no more than 3

9. Ask for a tour of the facilities so you can see the conditions in which the breeding stock and the kittens are kept

10. Do not purchase from any breeder that refuses to show you around and, similarly, avoid breeders who do not keep their stock in a clean and healthy environment

11. View the breeding stock to ensure that they are good examples of the breed and that they are healthy

12. Ask to see and interact with the kittens available for purchase

13. Spend a few minutes observing the kittens to see how they interact with one another and how they respond to human presence

14. Look around the facilities to make sure they are clean – if they are not, the kittens are unlikely to be healthy

15. Spend some time interacting with the kittens to determine their health and personalities

16. Give the kittens time to warm up to you before you attempt to handle them, then do so gently and carefully

17. Check the kittens for outward signs of ill health – the eyes should not be cloudy; there should be no discharge from the eyes, nose or mouth; and you should not see or feel any irritation or bumps in the skin

18. Ask the breeder about his policies regarding a health guarantee and what vaccinations the kittens will receive before going home

19. If all of the kittens look healthy, you can feel confident in making your selection (be aware that you will likely need to put down a deposit to reserve your kitten if he is not ready to go home that day)

It may take some time for you to narrow down your list of breeders and to make your selection, but it is definitely worth it. The more careful you are in selecting your kitten, the more likely you are to bring home one that is healthy.

3.) Considering a Rescue

If you are not concerned with breeding or showing your Siamese Cat, you may want to consider adoption. Adopting a cat is a great way to bring a new pet into your life without contributing to the growing problem of homeless pets. If you are considering adopting a cat, think about the following tips and statistics:

- Each year over 2.5 million adoptable pets are euthanized because there isn't enough shelter space to accommodate them

- Shelters provide all their pets with veterinary care, keeping them up to date on vaccinations and spaying/neutering all pets before adopting them out

- Adopting a pet is much less costly than purchasing from a breeder – a cat adoption fee is typically under $50 (£32.50)

- Shelter cats are already likely to be litter trained which saves you the hassle of doing it yourself

- Experienced shelter staff can help you find a pet with the perfect Siamese Cat personality to suit you and your family

- Adopting an adult cat saves you from the havoc young kittens can wreak in your house

- You will have peace of mind in knowing that you did your part to help provide homeless pets with a loving family

If you are considering adopting a Siamese Cat, check out one of these rescues or shelters:

Siamese Cat Rescue Center.

<http://va.siameserescue.org/>

Specialty Purebred Cat Rescue.

<http://www.purebredcatrescue.org/siamese-orientals>

RescueMe.org.

<http://siamese.rescueme.org/>

Siamese Cat Rescues Around the World.

<http://www.life-with-siamese-cats.com/siamese-cat-rescue.html>

SiameseRescue.org.uk.

<http://www.siameserescue.org.uk/homeswanted.htm>

4.) How to Select a Healthy Siamese Cat

Whether you purchase your Siamese Cat from a pet store, a breeder or a rescue you should take the time to make sure he is healthy before you bring him home. In many cases, spending a few minutes observing and interacting with the cat will be enough to identify any major health or behavioral problems. If you were to skip this step and take the cat home immediately, you could be saddled with expensive medical bills as well as a lifetime of dealing with a cat that has medical or behavioral issues.

Never buy a pet without seeing it in person first – do not take for granted the breeder's word that all of his stock is healthy because he may just be trying to make a sale. In order to ensure that you bring home a healthy kitten, follow these simple steps:

- If you are purchasing a kitten, look for one about 12 weeks old – he should be weaned by this point and will be just starting to become self-reliant

- Look at the kitten head-on to examine the fact, including the eyes, ears, nose and mouth

- The nose should be cool and damp without any signs of discharge

- The kitten's eyes should be bright and clear with no discharge – the third eyelid should not be prominent (if it is, it could be a sign of infection)

- Check to see if the kitten is cross-eyed – this fairly common in Siamese Cats of poor breeding

- The ears should be clean and sweet-smelling, no waxy buildup or odorous discharge

- Examine the body of the kitten – a swollen belly may indicate poor feeding or worms

- Check for indications of diarrhea both on the kitten and in the area in which he is kept

- Examine the coat – it should be smooth and glossy without any scaled or dry patches

- Watch the kitten as he walks – there should be no limp and the kitten shouldn't stumble or sway as he moves

- Pick up the kitten to see if it relaxes in your hold or if it tries to get away – a well-socialized kitten will be comfortable around people

- See how the kitten reacts to being startled – clap your hands and see if the kitten recovers quickly

Chapter Five: Caring for Siamese Cats

Compared to other pets, cats are fairly low-maintenance. You do not need to let them outside to do their business and they do not need to be taken for walks. This doesn't mean, however, that they require no care at all. In order to keep your Siamese Cat happy and healthy you must provide for his basic needs including safety, shelter, food and companionship. In this chapter you will learn how to provide for your cat's basic needs.

1.) Habitat Requirements

Unlike dogs and other household pets, cats are fairly self-sufficient. This does not mean, however, that you do not need to provide certain things for them. In order for your Siamese Cat to remain happy and health you should plan to provide them with the following basic necessities:

- Cat bed
- Scratching post
- Cat toys
- Food and water bowls
- Crate or carrier
- Grooming supplies
- Perch or cat tree

Cat Bed

Though your cat is likely to sleep anywhere and everywhere in your house, he may appreciate having a little space to call his own. A cat bed does not need to be extravagant, but something plush and comfortable will do nicely. You can even make your own cat bed by lining a cardboard box with old blankets or pillows.

Cat Toys

Siamese Cats are a very active and playful breed so you will want to have a variety of cat toys on hand. Many cats enjoy toys that make sound – a mouse with a rattle in it or a ball with a bell will be very popular. You can also find toys that consist of a stick and a feather attached to a string – these toys are great for playing with your cat. Cat toys vary in cost, but do not feel like you need to buy the expensive ones. In fact, you can make many simple cat toys yourself out of household objects.

Food and Water Bowls

In addition to providing your Siamese Cat with food and water, you also need bowls to put it in. If you walk down the aisles at your local pet store you are likely to see a wide range of products in this area ranging from simple metal bowls to decorative bowls and automatic dispensers. If you are on a budget, your best bet is to go with plain stainless steel bowls because they are easy to clean and inexpensive. If cost is not an issue, you may want to consider an automatic water dispenser that will keep your cat's water fresh and readily available.

Scratching Post

This is particularly important if you do not plan on declawing your cat. Cats, including Siamese Cats, have a natural instinct to scratch things as a means of sharpening their claws. If you do not provide your cat with a scratching post or similar item, you may find that he sharpens his claws on your furniture or tears up the carpet. To encourage your cat to use the scratching post as an alternative to your furniture, buy one that is infused with catnip or purchase catnip spray to use on it.

Crate or Carrier

As was mentioned earlier in this book, you will want to have a crate or carrier on hand for times when you need to take your Siamese Cat outside the house. There are several different types of carriers to choose from and the costs for each type vary. One of the easiest type of cat carrier to find is a hard-shell crate – these come in many different sizes so you can easily find one to accommodate your cat. Another option is the soft-shell carrier which you may be able to carry over your shoulder like a bag. These carriers are good for short trips, but a hard-shell carrier is recommended for long trips in the car for your cat's safety and comfort.

Perch or Cat Tree

Siamese Cats are excellent jumpers and climbers, so they will enjoy having a cat tree to climb on. Another option is to place various perches around the house – in many cases, tall furniture like bookshelves will fulfill this need. Some cat owners install special shelves on the wall simply to give their cats a means of observing things from on high. Buying cat trees from the pet store can be expensive, but if you perform a simple online search you will find that there are many easy ways to make them yourself.

Grooming Supplies

Siamese Cats have very short, glossy coats that do not shed as much as other breeds. This does not mean, however, that you can neglect to groom them. Brushing your cat's coat on a regular basis will help to keep it healthy and will also help to control shedding. To groom your Siamese Cat's coat all you are likely to need is a simple bristle brush. You may also consider a wire-pin brush because many cats like the way it feels.

2.) Feeding Siamese Cats

Your Siamese Cat's health is impacted by a number of factors, but diet is one of the most important. If you do not provide your cat with the nutrients he needs, how can you expect him to be healthy? Feeding your cat does not need to be difficult, but it does require a little more effort than simply picking a bag at random off the shelf at the pet store. In this section you will learn the basics about what your Siamese Cat needs in regard to his diet and how to go about providing for those needs.

a.) Nutritional Needs

The nutritional needs for adult Siamese Cats vary from those of kittens – while your cat is still young, he will need to be fed more frequently to support his growth. Young kittens should be fed small meals several times a day (about 4 times) whereas adult cats can be fed twice per day. For the most part, a high-quality commercial dry food will cover your cat's nutritional needs but you may want to supplement that diet with small quantities of wet food daily to maintain the health and texture of your cat's coat.

For specific details regarding the nutritional needs of your cat, consult the following chart:

Nutritional Needs for Cats		
Nutrient	Kittens, Pregnant, Lactating Cats	Adult Maintenance
Protein (g)	56	50.0
Fat (g)	22.5	22.5
Calcium (g)	2.00	0.72
Phosphorus (g)	1.80	0.64

Potassium (g)	1.00	1.30
Sodium (mg)	350	170
Magnesium (mg)	100	100
Iron (mg)	20.0	20.0
Copper (mg)	2.10	1.20
Manganese (mg)	1.20	1.20
Iodine (μg)	450	350
Vitamin A	250	250
Vitamin E (mg)	9.40	10.0
Vitamin K (mg)	0.25	0.25
Niacin (mg)	10.0	10.0
Folic Acid (μg)	188	188

Cats are naturally carnivorous animals, so the majority of their nutrients should come from meat-based sources. When shopping for commercial cat food, check the label to be sure that a high-quality source of animal protein is the first ingredient on the list. You should also pay attention to the name of the product. Consider the following when shopping for cat food:

- If the food is advertised with the name of a single ingredient (ex: beef), it must contain at least 95% of that ingredient

- Foods claiming to be made with two ingredients (ex: turkey and beef) must contain a combined 95% of those ingredients

- Foods labeled with words like 'dinner' or 'entrée' must contain at least 25% of the ingredient in the name (ex: beef dinner)

- Products that use the word 'with' in the name must contain at least 3% of that ingredient (ex: with cheese)

- If the product uses words like 'chicken flavor', it only needs to contain a detectable amount of that ingredient

- Good sources of animal protein to look for include beef, poultry, fish, turkey, chicken and other meat

- Many commercial pet foods contain grains but make sure that it is not the main ingredient

Another useful tip for finding a quality commercial cat food is to look for the American Association of Feed Control Officials (AAFCO) statement of nutritional adequacy on the label. This statement simply guarantees that the product meets the basic nutritional needs for cats in the life stage for which the product was formulated (ex: kitten growth or adult maintenance).

b.) How Much to Feed

To get a basic idea how much you should be feeding your Siamese Cat, check the instructions on the food package. All pet food packages must include feeding instructions, including an amount. While the energy needs of your cat may vary according to his size and activity level, these instructions will give you a good place to start. Make sure you are using the proper formula for your cat's age (ex: growth for kittens and maintenance for adults) then feed the amount suggested on the package. If your cat seems to be always hungry or is losing weight, slightly increase the amount of food. If he is gaining too much weight, slightly decrease the amount.

If you are curious to know exactly how much energy your cat needs on a daily basis from his food, you can calculate his resting energy requirement (RER) and adjust it for his activity level. To calculate your Siamese Cat's RER you can use the following formula:

$$RER = 30 \times [\text{body weight in kg.}] + 70$$

Take for example a 9-pound Siamese Cat – this weight would equate to 4.08 kg. Using the equation above, you would calculate RER = 30 x [4.08] + 70 which equals 192.4. For a neutered adult cat, you would then multiply this number by 1.2 for a total of about 231 calories per day. For an intact (non-neutered adult), multiply by 1.4 and for a kitten, multiply by 2.5.

c.) Foods to Avoid

For the most part, cats are not as interested in table scraps and human food as dogs are. This doesn't mean, however, that you do not need to be careful. <u>Below you will find a list of foods and plants that are poisonous or dangerous to cats</u>:

Onions	Chocolate	Fat trimmings
Garlic	Candy	Baby food
Chives	Gum	Macadamia nuts
Milk	Raw eggs	
Cheese	Bones	Persimmon
Alcohol	Dog food	Rhubarb leaves
Grapes	Liver	Salt
Raisins	Yeast	Tobacco
Caffeine	Xylitol	Raw fish

Chapter Six: Breeding Siamese Cats

Breeding your Siamese Cats can be a wonderful experience, but it is not something you should enter into lightly. If you are only interested in breeding for the purpose of making money, reconsider your motivations. Breeding cats involves bringing new life into the world – lives that you are responsible for – and it can be a lot of work. Only engage in breeding if you have healthy, quality stock to work with and if you are capable of caring for the kittens and providing them with good homes.

1.) Basic Breeding Info

Before you breed your Siamese Cats there are many things you need to think about. The first thing to consider is the health and genetic soundness of your cats. Siamese Cats in particular are prone to a number of congenital conditions, so you do not want to pass those conditions along to a new litter by breeding from unhealthy stock. Do not breed your Siamese Cats unless you have documentation regarding their own breeding to certify that they are free from congenital conditions.

Other things to keep in mind when breeding Siamese Cats include the following:

- Female Siamese Cats make excellent mothers so you are unlikely to have to hand-raise the kittens

- Queen Siamese (intact female cats) tend to go into heat more often than other breeds

- Siamese Cats tend to have fairly large litters, though 5 kittens is about average

- This breed often nurses the kittens for longer than other breeds – up to 12 weeks unless you wean them yourself

- Female Siamese Cats are capable of producing healthy kittens for as long as 10 years

- Male Siamese Cats are capable of siring litters throughout almost their entire lives – up to 16 years

a.) Sexual Maturity in Siamese Cats

You cannot breed your Siamese Cats until they reach sexual maturity. For most breeds, this occurs between 6 and 9 months of age, though it often happens earlier in Siamese Cats. Female Siamese are likely to have their first heat as early as 5 months of age – after this, they are capable of reproducing. Male Siamese Cats typically begin to produce sperm around 9 months of age and can be bred after they reach 1 year old.

The heat cycle is simply another name for estrus – a period during which the female cat is capable of and receptive to breeding. When a female Siamese goes into heat, she will exhibit swelling of the vulva along with a slight discharge. She will likely become very affectionate and vocal – you may be surprised at the big sounds coming from a small kitten. The estrus cycle typically lasts for around 1 week. If a successful mating occurs during this time, the female will go into a gestation period lasting about 63 days.

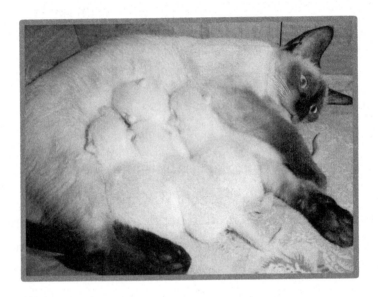

Fun Fact: During estrus it is possible for multiple matings to occur because it may take a few days for the female's hormones to settle down after breeding. This being the case, it is possible for a single litter of kittens to have more than one father.

b.) Summary of Breeding Info

Sexual Maturity (female): average 5 to 6 months

Sexual Maturity (male): 8 to 9 months

Breeding Type: polyestrous, multiple cycles per year

Litter Size: up to 13 (average 5)

Pregnancy: average 63 days

Kitten Birth Weight: 90 to 100 grams (0.2 to 0.22 lbs.)

Characteristics at Birth: blind, deaf, cream-colored or white

Eyes/Ears Open: 2 to 3 weeks, eye color will deepen/darken over time

Teeth Grow In: around 3 weeks

Color Points Develop: after 3 weeks or so, very clear after 8 weeks of age

Begin Weaning: around 7 or 8 weeks, mother may not wean naturally until 12 weeks

2.) The Breeding Process

Once your Siamese Cats have reached sexual maturity, all you have to do is wait for the female to come into heat. When a female cat is in heat, she will call loudly and produce strong pheromones that will be highly attractive to male cats. This being the case, it is essential that you keep your female cat indoors and tightly secured – you do not want to risk accidental breeding with any cat other than the intended stud.

For indoor cats, the heat cycle tends to coincide with the spring and summer. It is possible, however, for Siamese

Cats to go into estrus multiple times per year so you should be on the lookout for the signs. The first stage of the estrus cycle is called proestrus – this lasts 1 to 2 days and, during this time, the female may call and roll on the ground. She will not, however, be receptive to mating until she progresses into the estrus cycle.

Estrus lasts about one week on average and this is the time when you should bring the queen and the tom cat together. It is important that you bring the queen to the tom, not the other way around – a tom cat is more likely to breed if he feels comfortable in his environment. Choose your breeding location carefully and be sure to provide the tom with an escape route, as the female may respond aggressively after mating is completed. The mating itself should occur with little effort required on your part and it may only last up to 20 seconds.

Immediately following mating, your female Siamese will likely begin frantically grooming herself and she will not be receptive to any type of contact for about an hour. After this point, however, she will resume typical estrus behavior and will once again be receptive to mating. It is possible for several matings to occur during one estrus cycle. In fact, repeated breeding increases ovulation in the female.

If the mating resulted in conception, the female will go into a gestation period lasting about 63 days on average. If mating occurred but the female did not ovulate, she will go through a metestrus stage lasting between 5 and 7 weeks during which time she will show no reproductive behavior. Cats that are not bred during estrus will simply go through a 1-week period of rest before the cycle repeats. If the female becomes pregnant but aborts the litter, she will likely go into estrus again as well as 2 to 3 weeks later.

3.) Raising the Babies

In order to provide your pregnant cat with the care she needs, you should keep track of her pregnancy. To do this, you will need to make a note of the days on which she was bred and add 63 days to determine her approximate due date. Because you are likely to breed your Siamese Cat multiple times during her cycle, her due date may span the entirety of a week.

During her pregnancy, you can expect your female cat to gain about 20% of her body weight – approximately 2 to 4 pounds. Siamese Cats tend to become fairly plump in pregnancy, but they lose the weight quickly afterward to go back to their long, lithe shape. Offer your cat as much food as she will eat during pregnancy – cats do not tend to overeat during pregnancy so you do not need to worry about giving her too much food.

When your cat starts to approach her due date you should provide her with a nesting box – a safe and quiet place where she can give birth. If you do not offer your cat a nesting box, she will likely find a suitable place herself. When the due date is within 3 days, confine your cat to the room you want her to deliver in and make sure it stays dark and quiet. At this time you should begin to look for signs of labor which may include the following:

- Vomiting
- Panting or labored breathing
- Persistent licking of the abdomen and vagina
- Pelvic contractions
- Excretion of a small plug of blood
- Loss of interest in food
- Pacing the room while yowling

When your cat is ready to give birth, she will likely lay down on her side, squatting intermittently to expel the kittens one at a time. In most cases, Siamese Cats begin to give birth within one hour of the onset of labor. Once she begins giving birth, the entire litter should be delivered within 2 to 3 hours. After the kittens are born, the mother will clean them and chew off the umbilical cord. She will also likely start the kitten nursing before the next one is delivered. If she doesn't, you can gently place the kitten near one of her nipples to get him started.

After all of the kittens have been born, the female cat will spend most of her time nursing and cleaning them. You will see her licking the kittens to stimulate respiration immediately after birth and to help them urinate and defecate until they learn to do it on their own. It is essential that newborn kittens nurse from their mother within the first few hours of birth because this is when the colostrum is produced. Colostrum is the first milk a mother produces and it is full of vital nutrient and antibodies the kittens need to protect them until their own immune systems develop.

When Siamese kittens are first born, their eyes and ears are closed – they are also unpigmented, having white or cream-colored fur. It isn't until the kittens are 2 to 3 weeks old that they will begin to develop their color points, though you may see some color on the tips of the ears after 1 week or so. By 2 to 3 weeks of age, the kittens' eyes and ears will open, though it may take a few weeks longer for the iconic deep blue color of the Siamese eyes to develop.

For the first few weeks, your Siamese kittens will only nurse from their mother. By week 3, however, their baby teeth will start to grow in and they may begin to sample solid food. Siamese Cats tend to nurse their kittens longer than other breeds, but they should at least have begun weaning by 6 to 8 weeks. By 12 weeks of age the kittens should be weaned onto solid food and ready to be separated from their mother.

Chapter Seven: Keeping Siamese Cats Healthy

Responsible breeding and a healthy diet go a long way in ensuring that your Siamese Cat remains healthy. Even if you are careful with your cat, however, you cannot be sure that he will never get sick. In order to protect your cat, it is a good idea to familiarize yourself with the common health problems affecting this breed so, if your cat does get sick, you can make a quick diagnosis and start treatment. In this chapter you will learn about common Siamese Cat health problems as well as their symptoms and options for treatment. You will also learn how to prevent disease.

1.) Common Health Problems

Unfortunately there are a great many irresponsible pet breeders out there – this is particularly true for the Siamese Cat breed. If you breeding stock is not properly screened for congenital diseases, those same diseases may be passed along to the offspring and then on to future offspring. In addition to a number of congenital conditions, Siamese Cats are also prone to several other diseases. In this section you will find a list of common diseases affecting this breed as well as an explanation of the disease, its causes, symptoms and treatment options.

Common health problems affecting Siamese Cats include:

Amyloidosis	Feline Endocrine Alopecia
Cancer	Glaucoma
Cardiomyopathy	Hip Dysplasia
Dental Problems	Progressive Retinal Atrophy
Feline Asthma	Respiratory Problems
Feline Diabetes	Vestibular Disease

Amyloidosis

This disease results from protein deposits (amyloid) forming in the liver. These deposits often occur secondary to other problems such as inflammatory or lympho-proliferative disorders. As an example, conditions which result in the excessive production of white blood cells (lymphocytes) may actively lead to amyloidosis. This disease particularly affects Oriental breeds including the Siamese, Burmese and Abyssinian breeds.

Amyloid is a waxy, hard substance that accumulates in the liver and impairs its normal function. These formations may be the indirect result of the conditions mentioned above, or they could be caused by a familial immune disorder, a chronic infection or a tumor. Symptoms of amyloidosis include loss of appetite, sudden lack of energy, vomiting, pallor, yellowish skin, joint pain or swelling and head pain.

Unfortunately, there is no cure for amyloidosis but certain types of supportive care have been proven helpful. Blood transfusions and fluid therapy may be useful along with a modified diet to prevent further strain and damage to the liver and kidneys.

Cancer

Though cancer in cats may present in a variety of forms, the type most commonly seen in Siamese Cats are mast cell tumors. Also called mastocytomas, mast cell tumors are a type of skin tumor affecting the mast cells – a type of white blood cell that play a role in the immune system. Approximately 20% of all skin tumors in cats are mast cell tumors and over 90% of them are benign (not cancerous). These tumors are most likely to occur in middle-aged or older cats.

The cause of mast cell tumors in Siamese Cats is unknown, but it is thought that a mutation of certain genes may play a role. Common symptoms of this condition include raised hairless nodules on the skin, itching or redness and swelling. In some cases, mast cell tumors can spread to the internal organs, making it a visceral disease. When this happens, affected cats may show signs of systemic illness such as depression, loss of appetite and vomiting.

Treatment for this condition varies depending on the severity, though surgery is the most common option. Prescription of antihistamines may also help to alleviate symptoms of the disease.

Cardiomyopathy

The name cardiomyopathy refers to any disease that affects the heart muscle. Cardiomyopathy is the most common form of heart disease in cats including the Siamese Cat, and it is also the leading cause of heart failure. There are several different types of cardiomyopathy including hypertrophic cardiomyopathy (HCM), dilated cardiomyopathy (DCM), restrictive cardiomyopathy (RCM) and intermediate cardiomyopathy (ICM).

Hypertrophic cardiomyopathy is the most common form seen in cats and it is caused by an increase in the thickness of the muscular walls of the heart. This thickening then leads to a reduction in blood volume which causes the heart to get weaker and blood flow to the rest of the body is restricted. Unfortunately, the early signs of HCM are often missed and may not appear at all. Some symptoms may include increased heart rate, murmur, decreased appetite, coughing and weight loss.

The most common treatment for HCM is the administration of drugs that relax the heart muscle to increase its efficiency. Some cats may also require exercise restriction to reduce strain on the heart.

Dental Problems

For some reason, Siamese Cats have a greater risk of developing dental problems than other breeds of cat. Two of the most common dental problems seen in this breed are gingivitis and stomatitis. Gingivitis involves inflammation of the gums while stomatitis involves inflammation of the mucous membranes in the back of the mouth. Although the exact cause of these conditions is unknown, it is thought that some cats have an allergic reaction to bacterial plaque. It has also been suggested that certain diseases like feline leukemia and calcivirus may play a role.

Though the median age at which this disease develops is 7 years, there is also a juvenile onset form of the disease which can affect Siamese kittens between 3 to 5 months of age when their permanent teeth are just starting to erupt. Symptoms of this disease include irritability due to pain, reclusiveness, excessive drooling, difficulty eating and bad breath (halitosis). This disease can be diagnosed through an oral exam and treated with regular dental cleanings and good nutrition. A plaque-reducing water additive may also be recommended.

Feline Asthma

In Siamese Cats and other breeds, feline asthma is the result of chronic inflammation of the small passageways in the lungs. During an asthma attack, these passageways constrict which makes it difficult for the cat to breathe. This then results in respiratory distress which can become life-threatening in a matter of minutes.

Some of the common symptoms of asthma in cats including coughing, wheezing, rapid breathing, gasping for breath, gagging up foamy mucus, open-mouth breathing and blue lips or gums. Because asthma can be very dangerous, it is a good idea to seek veterinary care for your cat if you notice coughing or wheezing. Asthma may be caused by a number of factors including allergies, heart conditions, parasites, extreme stress or even obesity.

There is no cure for asthma in cats, though there are several options for managing it. Medications may be prescribed to help open the passageways in the lungs and to reduce inflammation. To prevent asthma attacks in affected cats, it is recommended that you avoid using strong perfumes or air fresheners and use a dust-free cat litter.

Feline Diabetes

This condition results from the inability of a cat's body to produce adequate insulin. When your cat eats and digests food, the nutrients are broken down into their most basic form – glucose molecules. Glucose is the main source of energy for the body and its presence stimulates the pancreas to produce insulin, a hormone which regulates the flow of glucose from the bloodstream into the cat's cells. If your cat's body doesn't produce enough insulin, he may have trouble utilizing energy and he may also develop very high blood sugar levels.

There are four classical signs of diabetes in Siamese Cats – ravenous appetite, increased urination, weight loss and increased water consumption. Feline diabetes can be diagnosed through a combination of physical examination and blood tests. Treatment for diabetes in cats typically involves dietary changes to stability blood sugar levels and to control weight in addition to insulin injections. In some cases, an oral hypoglycemic medication may also be prescribed by your vet.

Feline Endocrine Alopecia

This disease is a rare skin condition, the cause of which is unknown. Feline endocrine alopecia may result from an imbalance of hormones which leads the cat to groom itself excessively. This excessive grooming may lead to hair loss or the thinning of hair along with reddening and irritation of the skin. The area most commonly affected by hair loss is the abdomen and the inside of the hind leg region.

Diagnosing this condition can be difficult because the symptoms mimic several other conditions, including ringworm and other parasite infections. To aid in the diagnosis, the vet may prescribe a plastic cone collar to prevent the cat from grooming itself to see if the hair grows back. If this does not solve the problem, the vet will likely take skin scrapings to check for parasites or fungal infections.

Because the causes of this condition may vary, treatment for it can be difficult. Certain hormonal therapies may help to correct excessive grooming behavior and oral medications may help to stimulate hair regrowth. It generally takes 2 to 3 weeks for the hair to grow back.

Glaucoma

A disease of the eye, glaucoma results from increased pressure inside the eye. A cat's eye is filled with fluid (called aqueous humor) which contains the nutrients and oxygen needed to keep the eye healthy. When the pressure of this fluid builds inside the eye, caused by inadequate drainage, it may lead to degeneration of the retina and optic nerve which can affect your cat's vision. If not corrected, glaucoma can lead to partial loss of vision or even total blindness in severe cases.

Common symptoms of glaucoma include eye pain (rubbing or scratching at the eye), watery discharge from the eye, swelling of the eye, cloudiness of the eye and dilated pupils. It is important to treat glaucoma quickly in order to prevent irreversible damage to the eye. Analgesics may be prescribed to mitigate the pain and other medications may help to decrease inter-ocular pressure. In severe cases, surgery may be required, especially if blindness has already developed.

Hip Dysplasia

Though many senior cats develop mobility problems, Siamese Cats in particular are prone to joint issues. Hip dysplasia is a condition that causes the hip joint to develop abnormally which leads to the gradual deterioration of the hip joint. A healthy hip joint is composed of a ball and socket which fit perfectly together. Dysplasia occurs when part of the joint develops abnormally so that the ball and socket become dislocated.

Hip dysplasia is a congenital condition which means that it can be passed down from parent to offspring. This disease is more common in purebred cats and tends to affect females at a higher percentage than males. Common signs of hip dysplasia include decreased activity, difficulty rising, reluctance to run or jump, pain in the hip joints, decreased range of motion and loss of muscle mass in hind legs.

Hip dysplasia does not necessarily require surgical correction, as long as you catch it early enough. Physical therapy may help to loosen the joints while medications can help to manage pain. In severe cases, however, surgery may be the only option to prevent lameness.

Progressive Retinal Atrophy

This eye condition is a hereditary disease that commonly affects Siamese Cats. Progressive retinal atrophy, or PRA, results from degeneration of the photoreceptors in the eye. It is estimated that 33% of Siamese Cats are carriers for the disease and that 11% of them are actually affected by it. This is why responsible breeding practices are so important.

Progressive retinal atrophy is a non-painful condition and it may not result in any symptoms during the early stages. As the disease progresses, however, you may notice a change in the cat's personality and behavior, particularly at night (due to loss of night vision). Eventually you may notice dilation of the pupils, increased eye shine and cloudiness of the lens of the eye.

Unfortunately, no treatment for PRA exists and there is no way to slow its progression. In most cases, cats affected by PRA eventually go blind. For the most part, however, cats adapt well to blindness and they can live normal, happy lives if you make sure to keep their home environment stable.

Respiratory Problems

Siamese Cats in particular have an increased risk for developing respiratory problems. In addition to asthma, these cats are prone to upper respiratory infections which may be caused by one of two common pathogens. Calcivirus is an infection that typically lasts for a week and manifests in the form of nasal and eye discharge along with ulcers around the mouth and nose. Feline rhinotracheitis can last up to four weeks and it causes sneezing and drooling.

It is also possible for Siamese Cats to develop allergies to airborne allergens including dust, cigarette smoke, pollen, perfume and mold. Parasites like heartworm and lungworm may also contribute to respiratory problems in cats. Some common symptoms of respiratory problems include difficulty breathing, coughing, wheezing and sneezing. Because respiratory problems can be difficult to diagnose, your veterinarian may run a series of tests. The treatment for your cat's respiratory problems will vary depending on the cause of his distress.

Vestibular Disease

This disease affects the vestibular apparatus, or labyrinth, of cats. The labyrinth is a complex organ that plays a role in balance and orientation. Another name for vestibular disease is labyrinthitis. Common symptoms of this condition include problems with balance such as wobbling, circling, falling over and having trouble righting itself after a fall. Affected cats may lean against walls or crouch low to the ground when walking.

One of the most common causes of this condition is inner ear infection. Other possible causes may include stroke, head trauma, brain infection or drug intoxication. In Siamese Cats in particular a congenital form of the disease is common – this condition may manifest in kittens in the form of a head tilt or deafness. Unfortunately, there is no cure for this form of the disease.

When vestibular disease is caused by an inner ear infection, it often resolves itself in a matter of days. In more severe cases, treatment with antibiotics or antifungal medications may be recommended. During the recovery period, some cats may need assistance with eating and drinking.

2.) Preventing Illness

While providing your Siamese Cat with a nutritious diet will go a long way in keeping him healthy, there are other things you should do as well. One of the most important things you can do for your cat is to have him vaccinated. There are several vaccines that are required by law while others are simply highly recommended by most veterinarians. On the next page you will find a list of recommended vaccines for cats as well as a schedule regarding when they should be given.

a.) Core Vaccines for Cats

Core vaccines are those which are considered vital for all cats. These vaccines protect against panleukopenia (feline distemper), feline calicivirus, feline herpes virus type I (rhinotracheitis) and rabies. Rabies is the only vaccine that is almost universally required by law in the United States. In the U.K., the rabies virus has largely been eradicated.

Vaccine	Initial Vaccination	Booster Recommendation
Panleukopenia	6 weeks; every 3 weeks after until 16 weeks	1 dose second year then once every 3 years
Rhinotracheitis	6 weeks; every 3 weeks after until 16 weeks	1 dose second year then once every 3 years
Calcivirus	6 weeks; every 3 weeks after until 16 weeks	1 dose second year then once every 3 years
Feline Herpes Virus I	6 weeks; every 3 weeks after until 16 weeks	1 dose second year then once every 3 years
Rabies	single dose, as early as 8 weeks	Annually or every 3 years, depending on type of vaccine

b.) Non-Core Vaccines for Cats

Non-core vaccines are those which are recommended for some cats depending on their lifestyle. Certain vaccines such as the feline leukemia virus (FeLV) are only recommended for outdoor cats and for those that are exposed to other cats. The Chlamydophila vaccine is only recommended for cats that have been or are likely to be exposed to the disease.

Vaccine	Initial Vaccination	Booster Recommendation
Feline Leukemia	as early as 8 weeks, again 3 - 4 weeks later	annual
Chlamydophila	as needed	as needed
Feline Infectious Peritonitis	as needed	as needed
Bordatella	as early as 8 weeks, again 2 - 4 weeks later	annual
Giardia	as needed	as needed

Chapter Eight: Showing Siamese Cats

Showing your Siamese Cat can be both exciting and challenging. Keep in mind that cat shows are designed for purebred cats that conform to the standards for the breed – if you intend to show your cat, you may want to purchase a pedigreed cat from a reputable breeder. In this chapter you will find basic information about the Siamese Cat breed standard as well as an explanation of the different categories within the standard.

1.) Breed Standard

When it comes to showing Siamese Cats – or any breed of dog or cat – it all comes down to the breed standard. Also referred to as the bench standard or standard of points, the breed standard is a set of guidelines to which specimens of the breed are compared to judge their conformation. Breed standards exist not only for the sake of showing cats and dogs, but also to provide breeders with goals for improving their stock.

A breed standard typically covers the externally observable qualities of the animal – the physical appearance, the movement and the animal's temperament. For cats, however, breed standards focus primarily on physical appearance such as the shape of the head, structure of the body and the color. The main governing body for cats, the organization which publishes breed standards and runs shows, is The Cat Fanciers' Association, Inc. (CFA). On the next few pages you will find a breakdown of the Siamese Cat breed standard as well as a detailed explanation for each category of points.

a.) Breakdown of Points:

Head (20)

- Long, flat profile – 6
- Fine muzzle, wedge shape – 5
- Ears – 4
- Chin – 3
- Width between eyes – 2

Eyes (10)

- Shape, size, slant, placement – 10

Body (30)

- Structure and size – 12
- Muscle tone – 10
- Legs and feet – 5
- Tail – 10

Coat (10)

Color (30)

- Body color – 10
- Point color – 10
- Eye color – 10

Total Points = 100

b.) Explanation of Breed Standard

Below you will find an explanation of what features are considered in the assignation of points for each category within the breed standard.

General

The Siamese Cat is a medium-sized breed with a lithe but muscular form. Males may be larger than females, but still in proportion for the breed. The essence of the breed lies in its balance and refinement with all aspects coming together in harmony – too much or too little concentration should not be given to any one feature.

Head and Eyes

The head should be medium in size and in good proportion to the body. It exhibits a long, tapering wedge shape with the wedge beginning at the nose and flaring out to the tips of the ears. There should be no more than the width of one eye between the eyes. The ears are strikingly large and pointed, wide at the base. The eyes are medium in size and almond-shaped, neither protruding nor recessed. The nose is long and straight, the muzzle fine and wedge-shaped.

The chin and jaw are medium in size – the tip of the chin should line up with the tip of the nose.

Body

The breed is medium in size, having a long and graceful body. The bones are fine, the muscles firm, with a tight abdomen. The hips should not be wider than the shoulders and they should continue the same sleek lines as the rest of the body. The legs are long and slim with the hind legs being higher than the front. The paws are small and dainty with five toes on the front paws and four on the back. The tail is long and thin, tapering to a point.

Coat and Color

The coat should be short and fine with a glossy texture, lying very close to the body. Color on the body should be even with allowance made for darker color in senior cats. There should be definite contrast between the body color and color points. Points on the mask, ears, legs, feet and tail should be dense and clearly defined and all of one shade. There should be no ticking or white hairs in the points.

c.) Penalties and Disqualifications

During a cat show, the judges will compare the cat to the breed standard and assign points for how well the cat conforms to the standard. Throughout judging, points may be deducted for certain qualities – there are also certain qualities which may disqualify a cat entirely.

Penalties for Siamese Cats include:

- Improper color of nose or paw pads
- Soft or mushy body
- Protrusion of cartilage at the end of the sternum

Disqualifications for Siamese Cats include:

- Any evidence of poor health
- Weak hind legs
- Mouth breathing from nasal obstruction
- Visible kink in the tail
- Eye color other than blue
- White toes and/or feet
- Malocclusion – undershot or overshot chin

Chapter Nine: Siamese Cat Care Sheet

In reading this book you have learned all of the basics about Siamese Cats including where they come from, what makes them different from other breeds and how to care for them. There may come a time, however, when you need to reference a specific bit of information but you do not want to flip through the entire book to find it. That is where this care sheet comes in! Here you will find all of the facts and specifics about the Siamese Cat collected into one valuable resource for your convenience.

Chapter Nine: Siamese Cat Care Sheet

1.) Basic Information

Scientific Classification: *Felis catus* (domestic cat)

Size: medium-sized

Weight: 8 to 12 lbs. (3.6 to 5.4 kg)

Body Shape: long and lithe, graceful, triangular-shaped head and a thin, tapered tail

Coat Length: short, lies close to body

Coat Texture: fine, glossy

Shedding: low

Grooming: very easy, only requires brushing

Colors: four colors accepted by CFA – seal point, chocolate point, blue point, lilac point

Eye Color: deep vivid blue

Temperament: extremely affectionate and social, love being around people

Lifespan: average 10 to 13 years

Interaction with Children: gets along well with children, likes to play

Interaction with Pets: generally gets along well with cat-friendly dogs

General Health: higher rate of mortality compared to other breeds, several common diseases

Intelligence: very intelligent

Playfulness: very playful and active

2.) Habitat and Nutritional Needs

Basic Necessities: food/water bowl, cat bed, scratching post, cat toys, crate, grooming supplies

Diet Type: carnivorous

Amount to Feed: consult food package

Frequency of Feeding: 4 meals daily (kittens), 2 meals daily (adults)

Resting Energy Requirement: 30 x [body weight in kg.] + 70

Energy Needs: RERx1.2 (neutered adult), RERx1.4 (intact adult), RERx2.5 (kitten)

Types of Food: dry, moist or canned

Other Needs: constant access to fresh water

Dangerous Foods: onions, garlic, chives, dairy products, alcohol, caffeine, candy, raw eggs/fish, yeast, bones, dog food, etc.

4.) Breeding Tips

Sexual Maturity (female): average 5 to 6 months

Sexual Maturity (male): 8 to 9 months

Breeding Type: polyestrous, multiple cycles per year

Litter Size: up to 13 (average 5)

Pregnancy: average 63 days

Kitten Birth Weight: 90 to 100 grams (0.2 to 0.22 lbs.)

Characteristics at Birth: blind, deaf, cream-colored or white

Eyes/Ears Open: 2 to 3 weeks, eye color will deepen/darken over time

Teeth Grow In: around 3 weeks

Color Points Develop: after 3 weeks or so, very clear after 8 weeks of age

Begin Weaning: around 7 or 8 weeks, mother may not wean naturally until 12 weeks

Chapter Ten: Relevant Websites

Though this book is packed with valuable information about the Siamese Cat breed, you may find yourself craving more information about a specific topic. In this chapter you will find a collection of resources and relevant websites to provide you with a place to go when you are in need of additional information. Here you will find resources about Siamese Cats and cat care in general as well as links to pet supply websites where you can stock up on everything you need to care for your Siamese Cat.

1.) Resources about Siamese Cats

In this section you will find a collection of resources about the Siamese Cat breed. Here you will find links to websites full of information about the breed in general as well as specific resources for feeding and caring for these cats.

United States Websites:

"Siamese." The International Cat Association.
<http://www.tica.org/public/breeds/si/intro.php>

"Traditional Siamese Breed FAQ." Travels with Tigger.
<http://www.travelswithtigger.com/fanciers/trad-siamese-faq.html>

"Siamese Breed Standard." The Cat Fanciers' Association, Inc.
< http://www.cfainc.org/Portals/0/documents/breeds/>

"Siamese Cats." Catster.

<http://www.catster.com/cat-breeds/Siamese>

United Kingdom Websites:

"Siamese Cat Breed Profile." PetPlanet.co.uk.
http://www.petplanet.co.uk/cat_breed_profile.asp?cbid=18

"Siamese Cat Genetics." Siamese Cat Breeder.
<http://www.siamese-cat-breeder.co.uk/siamese-
cats/siamese-cat-genetics/>

"Siamese." Battersea Dogs & Cats Home.
<http://www.battersea.org.uk/apex/webbreed?breedId=11&
pageId=060-catbreed>

2.) *General Cat Care Information*

In this section you will find a collection of resources about general cat care. Here you will find links to websites full of information about breeding, feeding and caring for cats which you can apply to your Siamese Cat.

United States Websites:

"Cat Care Essentials." The Humane Society of the United States. <http://www.humanesociety.org/animals/cats/tips/cat_care_essentials.html>

"Caring for Cats." People for the Ethical Treatment of Animals. <http://www.peta.org/living/companion-animals/caring-animal-companions/caring-cats/>

"What you Need to Know About Feeding Your Cat." WebMD. <http://pets.webmd.com/cats/guide/cat-food-101-what-you-need-to-know-about-feeding-your-cat>

CatHealth.com. <http://www.cathealth.com/>

<u>United Kingdom Websites</u>:

"Cats." The Royal Society for the Prevention of Animal Cruelty. <u><http://www.rspca.org.uk/adviceandwelfare/pets/cats></u>

"Cat Diet." PSDA.org.uk. <u><http://www.pdsa.org.uk/pet-health-advice/kittens-and-cats/diet></u>

"Caring for Your Cat." Cats for Kids. <u><http://www.cats.org.uk/cats-for-kids/about-cats/kids-caring-for-your-cat/></u>

"Kitten and Cat Health." PSDA.org.uk. <u><http://www.pdsa.org.uk/pet-health-advice/kittens-and-cats></u>

3.) Websites for Cat Supplies

In this section you will find a collection of resources for cat supplies. Here you will find links to websites full of useful products including food and water dishes, litter boxes, cat food, toys and more.

United States Websites:

"Cat Products." Drs. Foster and Smith. <http://www.drsfostersmith.com/cat-supplies/pr/c/3261>

"Cats." PetSmart. <http://www.petsmart.com/cat/cat-36-catid-200000>

"Cat Supplies." ThatPetPlace. <http://www.thatpetplace.com/cat-supplies>

"Cat Toys and Supplies." CatClaws.com. <http://www.catclaws.com/>

<u>United Kingdom Websites</u>:

"Cat Supplies." Pet-Supermarket.co.uk. <u><http://www.pet-supermarket.co.uk/category/cat_supplies></u>

"Pet Medications." 1-800-PetMeds. <u><http://www.1800petmeds.com/></u>

"Cat Products." Total Pet Supply. <u><http://www.totalpetsupply.com/index.cfm/fuseaction/productcategory.cat></u>

Index

D

E

F

G

H

I

J

K

L

W

Acknowledgements

I would like to extend my sincerest thanks to my family for their patience with me as I spent endless hours researching and writing for this project. I would also like to thank Lucy, my own Siamese Cat and the inspiration for this book.

Photo Credits

Page 17 Photo By Vicvx via Wikimedia Commons, <http://commons.wikimedia.org/wiki/File:Siamese_cat_on_t he_island_of_Salina.jpg>

Page 18 Photo By St0dad via Wikimedia Commons, <http://commons.wikimedia.org/wiki/File:LuLu_s_eyes_by _St0DaD.jpg>

Page 19 Photo By Karin Langner-Bahmann via Wikimedia Commons, <http://en.wikipedia.org/wiki/Siamese_cat#mediaviewer/Fil e:Siam_lilacpoint.jpg>

Page 20 Photo By Syed Zillay Ali via Wikimedia Commons, <http://commons.wikimedia.org/wiki/File:Siamese_Cat_Fe male_2.jpg>

Page 23 Photo By Flickr user JamieinBytown, <https://www.flickr.com/photos/15609463@N03/6296608980 /sizes/l>

Page 34 Photo By BeltandPants via Wikimedia Commons, <http://simple.wikipedia.org/wiki/File:Seal_Point_Siamese_Kitten.JPG>

Page 38 Photo By Valerius Geng via Wikimedia Commons, <http://commons.wikimedia.org/wiki/File:Siam_blue_point.jpg>

Page 42 Photo By Martin Bahmann, via Wikimedia Commons, <http://en.wikipedia.org/wiki/File:Siam_Lilac_Point.jpg>

Page 45 Photo By Valerius Geng via Wikimedia Commons, <http://commons.wikimedia.org/wiki/File:Siam_lynx_point.jpg>

Page 48 Photo By Gean via Wikimedia Commons, <http://commons.wikimedia.org/wiki/File:Littlecatofmine.jpg>

Page 51 Photo By Arria Belli via Wikimedia Commons, <http://commons.wikimedia.org/wiki/File:Corrugated_fiberboard_scratch_pad_with_cat.jpg>

Page 54 Photo By Bodq via Wikimedia Commons, <http://commons.wikimedia.org/wiki/File:The_cat_without _a_name.jpg>

Page 58 Photo By Arantz via Wikimedia Commons, <http://commons.wikimedia.org/wiki/File:Siamese_kitten.jp g>

Page 61 Photo By Cindy McCravey via Wikimedia Commons, <http://en.wikipedia.org/wiki/Point_coloration#mediaviewe r/File:Neighbours_Siamese.jpg>

Page 64 Photo By S Zillayali via Wikimedia Commons, <http://commons.wikimedia.org/wiki/File:Siamese_Cat_wit h_her_Kitties.jpg>

Page 66 Photo By Kathy via Wikimedia Commons, <http://en.wikipedia.org/wiki/File:Siamesekittens.jpg>

Page 69 Photo By Flickr user Tigikrak, <https://www.flickr.com/photos/82072596@N00/275407367/sizes/o/>

Page 73 Photo By Pixabay user Steinchen, <http://pixabay.com/en/siamese-cat-cat-eyes-blue-fur-253735/>

Page 87 Photo By HawkSpirit via Wikimedia Commons, <http://commons.wikimedia.org/wiki/File:Siamese_Cat.JPG

Page 90 Photo By Louise Brown Van der Meid via Wikimedia Commons, <http://en.wikipedia.org/wiki/File:Siamese_cat_1960.jpg>

Page 96 Photo By Flickr user Zillay Ali, <https://www.flickr.com/photos/zillay/7302124444/sizes/l>

Page 101 Photo By Rick Truter via Wikimedia Commons, <http://simple.wikipedia.org/wiki/File:Two_Siamese_cats.jpg>

References

"Cat Breeding." PetEducation.com. <http://www.peteducation.com/article.cfm?c=1+2139&aid=891>

"Choosing a Healthy Kitten." WebMD. <http://pets.webmd.com/cats/guide/choosing-healthy-kitten?page=2>

"Common Medical Disorders in Siamese Cats." The Nest Pets. < http://pets.thenest.com/common-medical-disorders-siamese-cats-7325.html>

"Foods that are Hazardous to Cats." ASPCA. <http://www.aspca.org/pet-care/virtual-pet-behaviorist/cat-behavior/foods-are-hazardous-cats>

"Foods to Avoid Feeding Your Cat." PetEducation.com. <http://www.peteducation.com/article.cfm?c=1&aid=1029>

"Glossary of Feline Terms." Cat World. < http://www.cat-world.com.au/glossary>

Helgren, J. Anne. "Finding and Choosing a Purebred Cat Breeder." PetPlace.com. <http://www.petplace.com/cats/finding-and-choosing-a-purebred-cat-breeder/page1.aspx>

Hines, Ron. "The Stages of Feline Labor When Your Cat Gives Birth." 2nd Chance. <http://www.2ndchance.info/felinelabor.htm>

"How to Choose an Experienced Breeder." PetMD. <http://www.petmd.com/cat/care/evr_ct_cat_breeders>

"How to Choose the Best Cat Food." PetMD. <http://www.petmd.com/cat/slideshows/nutrition-center/choosing-best-cat-food>

"Now You're Talking Cat." CatChannel.com. <http://www.catchannel.com/kittens/yellowpages/article_cat_now_talking.aspx>

"Pet Vaccines: Schedules for Cats and Dogs." WebMD. <http://pets.webmd.com/pet-vaccines-schedules-cats-dogs?page=2>

Schindler, Melissa. "The Development of Siamese Kittens." TheNest. <http://pets.thenest.com/development-siamese-kittens-9785.html>

"Siamese." Cattime. <http://cattime.com/cat-breeds/siamese-cats#coat-color-and-grooming>

"Siamese." Hillspet.com. <http://www.hillspet.com/cat-breeds/siamese.html>

"Siamese." PetMD. <http://www.petmd.com/cat/breeds/c_ct_siamese>

"Siamese." The International Cat Association. <http://www.tica.org/public/breeds/si/intro.php>

"Siamese Breed Standard." The Cat Fanciers' Association, Inc. <http://www.cfainc.org/Portals/0/documents/breeds/standards/siamese.pdf>

"Siamese Cat Genetics." CatWorld.com.au. <http://www.cat-world.com.au/siamese-cat-genetics>

"Siamese Cats." Catster. <http://www.catster.com/cat-breeds/Siamese>

Singer, Jeanne. "Siamese Breeding – The Long View." CFA Siamese Breed Council. <http://www.siamesebc.org/yearbookArticles/yearbook79.html>

Smith, S.E. "10 Reasons to Adopt a Shelter Cat." Care2.com. <http://www.care2.com/causes/10-reasons-to-adopt-a-shelter-cat.html>

"Top Five Reasons to Adopt." The Humane Society of the United States. <http://www.humanesociety.org/issues/adopt/tips/top_reasons_adopt.html>

"Vaccines and Vaccination Schedule for Cats & Kittens." PetEducation.com. <http://www.peteducation.com/article.cfm?c=1+2143&aid=951>

"Vaccinations for Cats and Kittens." WebMD. <http://pets.webmd.com/cats/guide/cat-vaccinations?page=1>

"What Should I Look for in Choosing a Kitten?" Catster.com. <http://www.catster.com/cat-adoption/choosing-a-kitten>